Simple Thoughts

Simple Thoughts

Poetry for the Masses

Robert Tinajero II

Writer's Showcase
San Jose New York Lincoln Shanghai

Simple Thoughts
Poetry for the Masses

Writer's Showcase
an imprint of iUniverse.com, Inc.

For information address:
iUniverse.com, Inc.
5220 S 16th, Ste. 200
Lincoln, NE 68512
www.iuniverse.com

ISBN: 0-595-18002-7

Printed in the United States of America

This book is dedicated to those who have given me life,
physically, mentally and spiritually.

Contents

Acknowledgements

I would like to acknowledge those who have been an important part of my life. My parents, for giving me life and love, and for giving me the opportunity to do so much. My brothers and sisters for being there through all the fun and crazy times. My aunts, uncles and cousins for being part of a wonderful extended family. My friends, for being there and helping me enjoy some great times, especially David, Erika, Melissa, Sony, Vineet, Manoj, Roger G., Joe, Zach, LL, Fernie, Marissa, Gil, Dario, Missle, Roger, Joseph (nip) and Omega Delta Phi (Sigma). My teachers, for helping me grow mentally and spiritually, especially Ms. Oth, Ms. Herron, Mr. Sanchez, Rod Stewart, Bill Moore, Roy Melugin, Steve Stell, Dr. Howard, Dr. Power, Dr. Black and Dr. Skora. I would also like to thank the following for inspiring me to write, to think, to feel and to live: U2, George Herbert, William Shakespeare, Rumi, Martin Luther King, Jr., Tupac, Snoop Dogg, DMX, Kurt Cobain, Counting Crows, John Milton, Thich Nhat Hanh, Bede Griffiths, Matthew, Mark, Luke and John….

Introduction

Before I Begin

Many persons, both glossy and brash, have written many things on many occasions about poetry and poets. To look at poetry as a single entity is to kill it. To say "poetry is", or "poets are", is to bleed them of their life. At first, when I began to write my poetry, I was discouraged for I thought to myself, " I can never be Shakespeare ", but I have come to realize that the flip side to that is true as well. Shakespeare could never be me (this is not to say that I have the same poetic skill of shakespeare, but that my experiences are very unique and just as important).

These poems drip of shakespeare, herbert, faulkner, and other spirits who have come before me. These poems are for everybody, for "the masses." They are for those "educated" in the art of poetics, but also for those who know nothing of herbert or faulkner, and for those who even have difficulty spelling 'shakespeare', as I still do. Some poets have attempted to connect themselves with the liberal, with the marginalized, with the "commoners". They enjoy speaking of the noble savage, but forget that the "savage" part is false. They begin to feel more at home in book clubs, book stores and universities, with their big words, and slowly fade into a metaphorical "up". I am not fading or growing. Just writing. Writing.

My poems have been left dated so that you may see some of the feelings and thoughts I have had during the years I wrote them. Many of them correlate directly with experiences I had and others are just thoughts…simple thoughts.

I hope you can find something in these poems that connects with your own unique experiences. There are notes listed at the back of this book for some clarification on some of the poems.

Simple Thoughts

my poetry is everything, yet it is nothing. like me, it is simple in its complexity and complex in its simplicity.

2-17-97

❧ *[untitled 1]*

I'm drowning, and I wish I could swim.
Been floating for so long—it's sin.
Who am I, Where am I, and Where are We going.
My signs of despair are showing.
Need help, not much; just a soft shoulder.
Seasons are torpid, but I feel I'm growing colder.
My window, slowly cracking, tearing, bending.
Foul air is diluting, changing, whispering.
Help me roar like a lion but only change for the plus.
For when I come full circle, I want more than dust.

10-12-95

❧ *[untitled 1-revised]*

Drowning. Wish I could swim.
Been floating so long. It's sin.
Who am I and where are We going.
Signs of despair are showing.
Need help and just a soft shoulder.
Seasons torpid, but I'm growing colder.
My window cracking and bending.
Foul air diluting and changing.
Help me roar and change for the plus.
For when I come full circle,
I want more than dust.

revised 3-7-96

❧ *Spanish Moon*

Tempest mind and yearning heart
So young and so smart

Do I want this crimson moon
Whose arrival was just too soon?

Not in love or needing friends.
A desert rose who mends?

Not mars or saturn but earth in bloom.
Does my future lie on the Moon?

10-29-95

❧ *[untitled 2]*

Wake up! What are you doing?
Is it your lips or the world you're moving?
Why do you sit and read these words
When you should be flying with the birds?

Dreams are not only for the bed
Dream Outloud! is what the song said.

Don't merely accept notes into your head
But write a song before you're dead

One day into dust we return
Did the flame of your soul burn,
And leave scars on the face of the earth,
Or have you been a shadow since your birth?

Dreams are not only for the bed
Dream Outloud! is what the song said.

Don't merely accept notes into your head
But write a song before you're dead

11-4-95

❧ *Me?*

Probing knives
with endless strifes
produces not
silky webs for answers sought

Rusty metal does tear my heart
Loving questions reveal a chart

11-17-95

❧ *[untitled 3]*

with God as my wind
and you as my pollen
I live and I dream

12-5-95

❧ *Love*

To gaze at flowers, clouds and even rain
Yet to think of you

2-6-96

✌ *[untitled 4]*

I believe and hope
that in my grave
God and I
will be smiling

4-25-96

❧ *[untitled 5]*

violets red
and roses blue
in this crazy world
i still love you

7-96

❧ *like thunder after lightning*

i smelled of sweat and dirt
after a long days work
but you held me and kissed me
and lessened the hurt

you, i will follow

9-23-96

❧ *Torpid*

as i lie there, i cry there
with the sun outside my room
i see you, and i feel you
with "the rain is coming soon"

like a fire, like a liar
the arrow is a tomb
and the chosen, breathes a poison
for the day is not a'bloom

like the air, i am heir
to your want but not your need
or is it eye, is it i
who has fallen to my knee

now i grow, and i go
to the doorstep of the sea
"do not sink, do not think"
is the final plea

"do not leave", now i leave
with the holy spirit
and i rose, with a rose
torpid heart cannot give it!

10-11-96

✣ *AMDG*

i felt you in me as i knelt
your taste on my tongue is all i felt

i wanted to cry
for what was done
and what i had failed to do
looking up at the bleeding you

eyes in darkness
you are there
why so bothered
by their stare?

hair like wool
i heard your tune
like a dove
with all the love
of a father for his son
and i, dressed as brutus,
and not the faithful kent,
pierced the sun-lit sky
and cried out a lament

with my eyes and my senses
around you i build fences

don't know why
the snake is sly
and eats my loving trenches
and i try, but would die i,
would i die,

for your endless kisses?

11-7-96

❧ *to the dead*

i remember you
like footsteps
not on rock
but like those on snow
and your absence
like water

you
your absence
your love

not merely drops in the sea
but together
an oasis in the desert

11-26-96

❧ *A Poem from the Death Bed of Mr. Rob Bot*

i woke up
and saw the summer sky
in all its splendor.
it should have made me cry.
Instead
i marched.
was it left, right, left, right?
it must have been,
it always was.
birds chirped to my rigid stance.
my walk, they wished it were a dance.
i had no time to hear them,
much less feed them
like that Poor Old man.
he sat there.
what a horrid sight.
lofting bread at those noisy birds.
"go to work old man",
i felt like yelling.
but what good would my words do.
he was lost, in an odd world.
i was amused that he was smiling.
what a fake smile. he must have been proud.
he must have seen me coming. how couldn't he?

i was staring at his fake smile so long,
i hadn't noticed i stepped on something.
think it was a worm. damn thing.
now it's all over my shoe.

should have been in the grass,
where it supposed to be.

the end.

12-12-96

❧ *On the Eve of Something*

as i lit the candle
i lit your face
in that darkened cavern
i noticed
your beauty was not your youth
it is more than precious eyes
or silky hair
it is hope
it is life
it is you

my eyes
a cloudy prince
gazed
hoping and wondering
do i need you?
do i want you?
someday both

today

12-31-96

Marching towards and away

the Ides
the tides
the smell of rainy weather
in a time, in a place
of multi-colored feather
i wait
for a sign, for a time
for a note of hymnal pleasure

4-3-97

❧ *Slowly Climbing*

busy face with virgin skin
perched upon where you've been

looking forward to tilted mirror
i stand and wait for sign that's clear

birds do chirp and sing a song
i wished i'd heard it all along

piercing rings and friendly larking
fork the road of joyous harking

where are you and who am i
let's live the truth and not a lie

4-3-97

❧ *As you sit there i wonder*

your thoughts are wounded doves
in a crisp blueness of all and nothing
and your eyes, riddles of life,
hang, holding something
maybe wooden clocks
or not, or all, but something

4-3-97

Of thoughts unknown i speak

of thoughts unknown i speak.
the echo is not my yell,
or whisper. but then it is
and must be,
for words are thoughts,
and of this work
words are chained.

so to are wrists of saints
and thoughts so faint
as to not be heard, or harnessed
as they bleed

of nothing comes volcanic lips.
but someday in the past they will.

4-97

❧ *Once Divided*

music from waves,
not birds, are we

perhaps in time
my passion
will wash upon your sand
and flood
upon fleshy banks
and enter you fully

her stars unsparkled
neither transcend
nor live unearthed
as in yesteryear
when air met lung
and winter breathed
forming flakes of beauty
and uniqueness
out of nature's tears

4-11-97

Once were we and us, but now is i

your soul i want
my soul i give
feel me
steal me
let me live

loving lips, no search of blame
i give fully and want the same

4-11-97

❧ *perception of feeling lines*

behold a poem
its sacred words
in a vastness
of sounds and moans
for lips it has
and heart it holds
as one by one
the audience wakes.

fragile is this fragile world
so to our lives
and precious lines
or not, if all we know
is in our mind
for then these lines are all,
every grain
in every plain

4-15-97

❧ *i enter an exit within ourselves*

four, twenty, ninety-seven

i wept.
but so did she
in that un-sunlit room
as we talked
and split some bridge
made of brick
or maybe paper

we will see
what comes of rain
and flower
of sun and rose
of one who gives
and one who lives

4-21-97

❧ *retrospect*

i want your trust
as mirror has
and your thoughts
as kin of past

4-20-97

✢❧ *perched upon a weeping chair*

why is my love a foul smell,
a horrid thing,
a hound of hell?
does it scare thy beating heart,
scar thy hands,
and river part?

my love is real!,
and heart does feel.

i give you all,
stay and wait,
like ground in Fall,
yet you don't want
these open arms,
for thy soul they seem to haunt.

4-20-97

❧ *my ancient pillow friend*

my heart,
a death row bed,
is numb
with thoughts of ice,
and rage,
and horrid plague.

its roots, seep
deeply into loving ground,
soil rich and soil red.
a redness much like
that of bleeding scars,
loving cards,
and mother's lips—
those lips that love,
but fade away
with birth of other needs.

4-22-97

❧ *this bird does fly alone*

my partner,
she fades,
into tall trees
and thick grass
with only spots
of light, of sight,
allowing me to catch
a hope, a glimpse,
of times gone by
and times to come
in a world undone
by riddles
and aching hearts

a fading,
both dim
and bright
(depending on the magician heart),
that still cages
my peaceful eye
and numbing heart.

4-23-97

❧ *via San Teodoro*

in this maze
of thoughts,
dreams,
hopes,
and tears
i live,
encaved,
with only the same
as my lantern,
and You my fuel,
and you my flame.

4-23-97

❧ *coming upon a fork in the road*

i have followed
waves and currents
despite my lucky mind
but someday
my hope
is to preach,
unlike the Pharisee,
of a trek
that neither
beats the beaten path
or beats the path less beaten,
but rather unearths
a golden trail—
a gold brightened
not by multitude,
but by the glimmering face
of love, imagination,
faith and mind—
a trail laced with
idealism and
built upon, both a base
of determinism
(soft as mothers hands),
and a repellence
of ignorance.
a trail,
unbeaten,
burning softly
from doric

to corinthian,
then back
to a more complex
simplicity.

4-23-97

❧ *[untitled 6]*

spread upon a falling horse
beneath the fading sky
i set upon a faithful course
learning clouds do cry

heading south in youthful bliss,
yearning for some destination,
i stumbled upon a natural kiss
a holy sign of God's creation

'twas not a snowy dove
nor a birthing hare
for it was truly love
'twas a dieing grizzly bear

begun 5-1-97

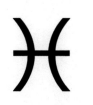

❧ *an impression*

perhaps in a world
swimming,
in color, in shades,
in monet,
you can love me.

my world searches
for a canvas
brushed by hands,
tears and simple things,
an existence dripped upon
by white,
as raindrops do to redwoods,
violets and dieing weeds.

5-7-97

❧ *[untitled 7]*

i dwell in clouds,
black and wet,
waiting for the sun to rise
more than it already has.

4-97

❧ *[untitled 8]*

i sit, moving,
reading revelation,
living it
grasping white beards
and baby tears
and thoughts on
rails
coming
and going

Born in the sun was i,
by ironies hand
in a half-full glass,
nourished by love
and faith,
(faith: the chameleon)
the latter crawling,
from eyes to brain
on a rusty track
on the sand of time.
Then came the sweet smile
of education, in walls of brick,
with its piercing teeth
and half-questioned knowledge.
It was death, it was life.
What a power, a force,
like nature's river
and man's religion.
i must applaud.

4-97

❧ *empty*

in a world of many
i am empty
but not alone
in my loneliness

to you i cry
as if in the cavern
of my mind
hearing echoes
of voices,
or noises,
in search
of an island
where we can dwell.

i am not inspired.

5-27-97

❧ *mine eyes have seen*

duceo

we have begun our walk
unknowingly
or should i say
you have joined my march
for i see a path ahead of me
that grows smaller
as it cuts the green fields
and brownish roots
blanketed by voices,
visions
wrapped around eyes,
bone, blood and breath
which walk ahead,
along and behind

walk with me
hold my heart and i will lead you

moneo

you can blur
into my landscape,
as many have,
or walk beside
grasping hand,
back to back,
on this journey sacred
of burning flames
and wooden canes

5-29-97

Ω

❧ *[untitled 9]*

sitting on the deck
like a golden eagle
were God-Spirit-Son,
the three, aboard The Beagle

finished 10-24-97

❧ *sunlight on my face*

you didn't call
again
in this midnight hour
of pain and flower
as i try to live without
within

melting water
feeds my soul
in this passing time
as only my
closed eyes see you
and open dreams
steal you from other parts
placing
you and i
in a ship at sea
loaded by golden riches
sinking us
hoping
that our love has wings
as Icarus sings

7-3-97

❧ *Rain*

in this world of roots and branches
there is no search of other

as my soul needs a friend
my heart needs a lover
as my eyes need a light
my brain needs a mother

7-8-97

❧ *The sky beats on your back as the sun is turning blacK*

you say it's midnight
as the sun beats on your back
you tell me to be smiling
as the sky is turning black

oh how i miss you
or at least who you were
dancing in the Magi clouds
with me holding myrrh

oh how i waited
for you to find your way
sitting in the starry sky
praying for that day

oh how i'm lost
in this desert sphere
searching for open eyes
overflowed in frigid tear

you say it's midnight
as the sun beats on your back
you tell me to be smiling
as the sky is turning black

7-29-97

❧ *once*

need to go to Chile
and have myself Eleven
i hear it never rains
while in that liquid heaven
maybe then i'll forget
all that we have been
and turn myself over
to the dancing city sin
or
maybe i'll remember
all that we have been
look at the frowning moon
and wish it were your grin
then i'll waste all weeks of seven
buy a home in Chile
and have myself Eleven

9-3-97

✸ *goodnight, not good morning*

she said
"i'm too sleepy" as
she woke up and
walked out my door
and i
trying to un-puzzle her
kept dreaming in my
lively sleep of
the last…
of the past we shared

how can you walk away
as if….
but it did and will
or won't
who knows?
He, me or them
not you because
you show the
unsaid side of lips
yours
our….

myself and others
you

9-6-97

❧ *bondage*

"I want freedom!",
cried the son of Zion
as the deep sea split,
as *moksha* hit.
"I want freedom!",
cried the darkened Lion,
as the chains were torn
and liberty born.
"I want freedom!"
were mothers, daughters cryin'
as walls were broke,
as lit Eve spoke.

how glorious!
those three words,
in times of hate
they are uncaged birds

but now, with love
as our cell and chain
these three words
bring no flower
to my rain

9-19-97

❧ *Fourteen Lines in Iambic Pentameter*

Contained are thoughts and words within my mind
Which long for flight beyond these walls doth built,
For it rains chains of meter and of rhyme
Which pierce this holy place of hope and silt:
Fields of flowers are fenced by wicked crime
As roads and verse are locked by whips of guilt
And clouds and birds are asked to march in line.
But oh! i hear the lovely tempest wind.
In this time, this line, Volta does now speak:
"Go now, go north, go walk atop the earth,
Which lies beneath the watery red sea,
And sing and see the bells that freedom ring.
Unwed the hold, the lock and bolt, and run…."
(Two weeks have come, now my words must be done.)

finished-9-29-97 for Bill Moore

❧ *[untitled 10]*

draped in your smell
i can hear you blink
and feel your heart beat
on my lips
as we speak,
without uttering a sound,
and sleep
for days,
knowing this is not a dream,
holding rays
that leap
over holy mounds
and leak
onto ships
at sea that meet,
at the golden brink,
your heaven and your hell

10-7-97

❧ *To touch and to Feel*

as i invoke a simile
of you and me
i remember touching you,
your skin,
in ecstasy
as a blind man
feels the braille
of a Shakesperean sonnet
on his soul

10-12-97

❧ [untitled 11]

my ice did melt
for a sec or two
as we danced
within the glance
of me and you
but you are there
and i here
as i hear their
shouts of sweet despair
which call for me
to bend at knee
and wake from this unburning sleep
and make mends with fallen sheep
so i can see
the light of night
and dark of day
which feeds my soul
and places Thee
in my lap and in my soul
and thus brings forth
amongst the earth
a life which lives
buried beneath the soil
of lady silt
of holy guilt

11-12-97

❧ *YOU!....and me*

your coat did never hide
as you stood in rain outside
you never let you cry
as your mother laid coffin by
you never prayed a hymn
as others preyed with sin
you always walked on by
as the beggar gave a try
you always turned your head
as the victim felt her dread
you always prayed a hymn
as you wanted help from Him

11-12-97

❧ *nice breeze*

thank you, i say
for being a friend
for being a mend
in this world where sometimes we are lost
i thank you, i do
for not speaking
too much
and making the moment
just right—
for listening, and sometimes
just hearing
to what i had and have to say
and i thank you for looking at me
that way
that day
and for holding my hand
and for holding my hand

11-25-97

❧ *black, ink, hole*

writing about writing
i thought
was the easy way out
as i dragged time and space about
with my gravity
and insanity

but it is not
i know
for the ocean speaks of water
and the sun of his father
as i end to write
as i pen my might

12-1-97

❧ *POW*

strange
like speaking to someone in the same room
without looking them in the eye
am i
feeling

lonely
like a single budding rose
amidst the dry of the desert
am i
living

caged
like an odd-talking genius
in an un-padded mad house
am i
thinking

free
as i turn this fourth key
in this room of reason
am i
running

12-7-97

❧ *Zion to Bethlehem*

i would cross the river
filled of melting dross
only if you were the light
in my exodus

i cross wood and shiver
for now is the loss
of that heavy coat of spite
which drowns all of us

12-97

❧ *From Ash to Dust*

from ash to dust
run all of us
without a fuss
yet i
want to stop
and wet thy dust
with loving rain
for at least
a fleeting moment
and breathe thy ash
and with cupid clash

1-30-98

❧ *true Love*

i could compare thee to the month of may
and tell thee that with you my soul will always stay
i could search through my mind and say,
like water in a rose, *in te domine*
but instead
i tell you that i know
i know i will be there when you are ill
with spit and vomit on the floor,
when your bloody nose drips
onto dirty hands
and you smell like morning
or sweaty feet

there, next to your hospital bed,
i will clean your piss and shit,
kiss your sweaty hand,
feed your drooling mouth.
through all the mud and roses
i must not just move these lips
but also move these hands,
And this i will do
For in truth, i love

2-18-98

❧ *you know not*

you think you know me
the notes in my head
the girls in my bed
but
you don't understand
my noble savagery
my complex imagery
impressionistic mastery
and religious tapestry

you think you see me;
the clothes on my back
the tongue in its sack
but
you don't understand
my world view stance
my complex prance
idealistic dance
and simple glance

you think you feel me;
the life in my soul
the fill of my hole
but
you can't understand
my sight of life
my complex strife
heavenly wife
and juliet knife

2-24-98

❧ *out of gold*

up-right, eyes bright
walking
towards floors of marble, doors of bronze
scent of glory and micheal's story
turn
struck
bernini's buzz casting shadows on gold and wooden chair
no time to stare
left, down, gold, paint
up, right, peter, saint

thoughts of God
behind the column He must be
there, no
up, up, latin tongue
scent of church and maybe mass
back, grand, wet thy hand and cross thy head
bells, and bells, and incense, bells
above the tune, besides the holy pool
there is He
no and nay
where does my Lord stay?

out, drained, scented
wet
down-looking, heavy steps, short and drown
drag
eyes lift
poor man, sewer man, hand to pocket
extended arm, thrice rounded-gold
now silver to shiver, poor to poorer

Simple Thoughts

eyes bright
hidden no longer, is God, is God, is God

3-6-98

chant more of venus

through the lands and the tongues
he brew a cup of light-in-night
to see the shores of his lady, laden lake
and there his eyes-surprise was she
laced in grace and trickery
so thus he chose the golden gloss
becoming one with foolish loss

i
mine self in humble-noble basket
claiming one-third silver casket
with one hand held her printed face

the other still holding fleshly grace

3-12-98

✣ *epic*

blue-bird stance casting shadows on winter's coat
   boast, boast—the boat does shave
with a 'blip', 'blip' waving swim
   and an uncertainty
notes, and notes and letters with sounds
slowly plundering through the up-most strategy
down, now—rolling
   slip, slip, quick
past those fast and small and fast too, tundra slopes
muddy banks under the underneath earth, worn
   now and dead

dammed river

4-13-98

❧ *[untitled 12]*

sadness abounds
with help of three-pronged reflections
of flickering candle flame
and a stormy night that knocks at window pain;
unanswered except for the broken glass
and shaking house

alive, barely,
and balled in

balled into a thinking game

5-9-98

❧ *write to right*

want
wanting to shoot
the canon
its men and marchly march
with bows of barrios, slums
deep-down disease
and life.
that down-run down-town
rock and roll life

5-28-98

❧ *[untitled 13]*

you say all i want
is to talk about the weather
but don't realize it's the coast
and it's september

it's always that season
don't you remember?

9-24-98

❧ *i am*

little i am i
but yet an i
divided by the real and the Real
the Form and the now
the mind and the plow
learning to unlearn
what a funny thing—a paradox that may not exist
as i sit and run and sleep awake

a child in water
a priest in vegas
to hope they take us

child in water
buddha with fly-swatter

10-6-98

❧ *christian meditation*

the crisp joy of now, with tears and notes of music
strolling down my slow cheeks, surrenders a sense
of minute greatness—an inward glowing as soul
and mind and body dance as one, an outward glowing
as 'my' and 'mine' and 'you' mingle as do sun and flower,
minute and hour,
brick and tower.
a greatness and a now at the core of reality, which are distant,
which i ask myself to find then ask Him to bind.

10-20-98

✒ *answer me*

what if i told you i stopped eating meat
because i'm not a cannibal
what if i told you i loved all strangers
as much as my mother
what if i told you that i am empty
and thus truly full
would this bother you,
your thought of me?

what if i told you i'm going to be silent
because i have knowledge
what if i told you i want to die
for i'm infinite and divine
what if i told you i loved you
before and after you hit me

would this bother me,
my thought of you?

11-4-98

✤ *[untitled 14]*

information brings dazzling waters
as waves enter dry quarters
and wet
what was once dry and damp—comfortably cold
and water plants and words
vines, thorned and sweet

i'm trying to remember what i learned
while forgetting what i heard

i'm scared
yet more comforted than ever

11-30-98

❧ *princess visit*

coming full circle
i stand where we began
no longer just a pawn
but controller of my plan

….scents and scenes
with white limousines
a touch, a look
a kiss, a hook
a prince in charge
of controlling me
a rhyme that's off
a mind that's lost
a poem that just doesn't know

i'm embedded

2-22-99

S

❧ *Thing*

this stretch of road
goes past the soul
and helps me touch the world.
i begin to learn
the most specific word
we have is Thing.
not House or Chair
or Bird or Bear,
or even Love and Soul.

what i want and feel from life
no word can bring
except a feeling and a Thing

3-10-99

❧ *Journey*

we must move from reality to Reality
from love to Love
from truth to Truth
then we can die from death.

3-31-99

❧ *earthly love*

my cane
but not my crutch
are you,
for one allows me to walk,
the other,
helps me walk better

3-31-99

❧ *America's Prayer 1999*

our father
who art in heaven
hollowed be our name
thy kingdom come
our will be done
on heaven as it is on earth
give us this day our daily Benz
and forgive us our trespasses
and lead us not into temptation
but deliver us from evil. aMen

1-11-00

❧ *ten 'till two*

you give me the type of call
i've gotta take in the other room
you tell me words about how
you're coming soon
about how where you're from
it's almost noon
about the time we kissed in the rain
when birds flew away
with our pain
about the twelve o'clock train
that you're not on
that you're not on

1-21-00

mirror

and i'd like to be a mirror for the son
and i'd like to be a mirror for the One
my skin my tool
to hide the fool
who yearns for just one thing

in the dirt and alley ways
where hate does stay
and greed does pay
i'd like to be a mirror to the One

with Him and El-Ohim
singing happy hymns of joy,
"you see that boy
you see my boy,
he is a mirror for the one"

2-00

❧ *Rosa and Hagar*

With shades of the 60's
I walk to my home
60 and shaded
I walk all alone

And now I can ride
The front of the bus
But only because
I have no car,

And now I can enter
Where I'd like to eat
But it hides not
My age-old scar

Thrown to the streets
With child in hand
I'm wandering, I'm pondering
This colorless land

Where is the Lord
Who will send his sun?
Where is the Lord
Who will hear my son?

With shades of the 60's
i walk to my home
60 and shaded
i walk all alone

4-17-00

❧ *Gray*

i'm gray and old
and not so bold
but bright with thoughts of now and next
gone up the steps
atop the slide
but now i feel the young hands push

i'm wise and green
a lot i've seen
teaching and learning all at once
rose from the ground
and blossomed still
but now i feel the young hands push

let me live
let me give

let me die

let me give

let me live

5-3-00

❧ *gone fishin'*

i'd like to fish-hook heaven
and reel it down to earth
i'd like to grab Almighty
and rub Him in the dirt

i'd like to help you understand
He's not only in the light,
but walks among the shadows
that talk to us at night

5-24-00

❧ *[untitled 15]*

though fullness and emptiness
are two in the same,
nosferatu lies in between
and smiles and laughs
and weeps much too
for he's lost and found
at just the same time

hearts of darkness
and souls in the dark
may not live in the chest
but in the mind
may rest

7-5-00

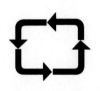

❧ *[untitled 16]*

caught between the dollar and the heart
living without living in the belly of the dark
we stand and run in a room of chairs

we stand and run in a room of chairs

9-29-00

❧ *greed and envy seep in the room*

the world a room
and us the groom with no filter
and no broom
as we watch the mirror
then watch the cage
thinking the mirror
has no rage

then catch a glimpse of heaven
a glimpse of hell
but don't point fingers
at ourselves
as we rub our eyes
and squint at fog
pointing at the speck
but ignoring log

9-29-00

❧ *[untitled 17]*

in the dark of night
when the sky is no longer blue
comes the green of money
comes the red of Nosferatu

9-29-00

EvolutioN

in your car and home
with your clock and phone
in your work and play
with your night and day

what have you done
to differentiate yourself
from a monkey?

9-29-00

✤ *[untitled 18]*

you wonder
around my streets at night
and laugh and smile
and play your part
you dance around the edges
the edges of my heart

you drive all night
and come around
the edges of my little town
but you don't realize
your phone is always upside down

it's always upside down

10-15-00

❧ *To George Herbert*

.your labor is not lost
for in God i do me store
i good to myself, the poor
and build without much cost
a house of old in my mind
and chance for Him to find

To His Success

Robert Tinajero II

A great silence overcomes me,
and I wonder why I ever thought
to use language.
　　　　　—Rumi—

Notes

Untitled 1: Torpid means to be inactive, much like an animal during hibernation.
Untitled 2: The song referred to is "Acrobat" by U2.
AMDG: AMDG (Latin)—*Ad Magnus Deus Gloria*, For the Greater Glory of God. Brutus and Kent were both characters in Shakespearean plays. Among other things, Brutus was known for his betrayal and Kent for his loyalty.
Slowly Climbing: Larking–playing. Harking–listen closely or refer to.
Via San Teodoro: Via San Teodoro is a street in Rome, Italy.
Coming Upon a Fork in the Road: A Pharisee was a type of Jewish priest who was many times labeled as a hypocrite in the New Testament. Doric and Corinthian are different architectural styles of columns, with Doric being very simple and Corinthian being more stylish and complex.
An Impression: Monet was an artist know for his impressionist style.
Mine Eyes have Seen: *Duceo* (Latin)–to lead. *Moneo* (Latin)–to warn.
Untitled 9: The Beagle was a ship which carried Charles Darwin.
Sunlight on My Face: Icarus is a character whose wings melted when he flew too close to the sun.
The Sky Beats on Your Back as the Sun is Turning Black: The Magi is one of the wise men who visited baby Jesus with gifts, including myrrh.
Once: *Once* (Spanish)–eleven. *Once* refers to a drink that is commonly taken in the country of Chile.
Bondage: The son of Zion refers to Moses. *Moksha*–liberation.
Fourteen Lines in Iambic Pentameter: Fourteen lines written in iambic pentameter is the typical form for a sonnet. Volta is a term used to describe the line in the sonnet which changes/shifts the poem.
True Love: *In te Domine* (Latin)–In you I live.
Out of Gold: Refers to a visit to the Vatican.
Chant More of Venus: Gloss–box.
Mirror: El-Ohim is a name used for God in the Old Testament.
Rosa and Hagar: Rosa refers to Rosa Parks and Hagar is a character in the Old Testament who was left to die with her son out in the wilderness.
Untitled 15 and Untitled 17: Nosferatu is Dracula.